All rights reserved, no part of this publication may be either reproduced or transmitted by any means whatsoever without the prior permission of the publisher

VENEFICIA PUBLICATIONS UK

*Typesetting © Veneficia Publications UK
March 2021*

I was happy to hear from Diane of Veneficia Publications UK that she was able to publish this book of Martin Pallot's poetry, following his untimely death in July 2020. Martin passed too soon for a soul full of poems and stories yet to be told and as a friend and colleague, a kind and thoughtful man, he is still sadly missed. We are fortunate to have the consolation of the words he left behind.

Martin was an incredibly talented wordsmith; his poetry takes you to another place, one where nature borders the otherworld. Martin was himself a "green hearted man" with "a woodland wisdom" (as he describes Puck), frequently visiting his beloved Epping Forest. His poetry has a depth that comes from not fearing the dangers of wandering off into a "darkling wood", an evocative allure from his ability to see the beauty in everything and a charm in paying tribute to the 'small things', (even a dead bee lying on the pavement).

The poetry in 'Around the Corner of my Eye' is arranged in the order of the seasons, from spring to winter, ending with the poignant beauty of the final poem 'Afterword'. The end of the book has space for your own thoughts and inspirations after you have immersed yourself in the magic of his words. Do write on it. He would want you to. And you will certainly be inspired.

June Kent, editor, Indie Shaman magazine

ACKNOWLEDGEMENTS
(and a dedication)

Firstly, sincere thanks to Veneficia Publications UK for their good humour, help and advice as well as for taking the risk (again!)

Secondly, many thanks also to June Kent at Indie Shaman Magazine where some of these pieces first saw the light of day.

And lastly (but not leastly) and 'cos I promised, this book is dedicated to the Cats ....

Tiger (who taught me respect for my fellow mortals) Pushka, Bagpuss, Machka, Baloo, (who definitely knew the bare necessities of life) and Scrappy.
Purrrs n snugz to each and all.

And to Mick, the Dog, who is not forgotten neither.

ALL ROYALTIES FROM THIS BOOK GO TO BATTERSEA DOGS AND CATS HOME.

Thoughts and Fancies.

When I was at school I was, according to my teachers, only any good at three subjects: English, History and I quote, "Staring out of the window and letting his mind wander" (usually, the latter was followed by a large exclamation mark!)

However, they are still my favourites, although history has become more myth and folklore and these days, I'm just as likely to be sitting under a tree as looking out of a window.

In fact, I think my abilities in "wandering" might even have improved now I no longer have irate men in bat wing capes hurling bits of chalk and interrupting my wonderings.

For you see, I have learned, that I am a most unapologetic Pagan Romantic.

My eye is always drawn to the buttercups that glow beside a woodland path and my mind is always drawn to wonder just who might wander, by their light, beneath the silence of the Owls wing; or I'll see a pudding stone beside an old straight track and start to dream of how it came to be associated with a certain "Goodman Green" or of the whirl of stars and other wonders it might have seen. Then again, I'll stand and stare into the wooded tangle of a bramble bush as the sunlight shifts shadows and my fellow mortals scurry and buzz and I'll imagine the generations of small lives that patch has known, the dreams and stories that it might hold, protected far better than Sleeping Beauty ever was.

Although, as you will see, I still find Bat wings a bit of a worry!

FORWARD

*Those folk
who go for a day in the country,
then don't even try
to get out of the car.
But simply sit, as if
this is as far
as they dare to go.
With windows shut
and music on 'blare.'
They just sit and stare
like frightened rabbits,
at the glare of that big
headlight in the sky;
picnicking on diet coke
and fag smoke.
Then they leave
the leafy ash
tray lay by,
and curse the traffic
as they try
to get back home.
In time to sigh
at 'Springwatch' on T.V.
but really cannot see
why people make a fuss
about the country.*

AROUND THE CORNER OF MY EYE

BY

MARTIN PALLOT

SPRING

Goddess,
Walking the earth,
Longing for her stag love,
Pulse of oak within her green blood,
Rising.

ON THE HILL

Halfway down the hill
And the mist blows back,
To reveal
The lord of the vale.

Vapour trails
Trickling from antler tips,
Hooves lost
In a waded froth of frosted turf.

Diamond dancing flanks
Flicker, as he takes my scent;
The blood rushing breath
Of fight or flight.

There is a level stare
That seems to say,
"This I could do!"
And a stamp of hoof
That crushes me, in absentia,
Beneath the shards of grass.

Then the bow of his back unbends,
And sends him curving Away;
To vanish again
Across the swirling,
Otherworldly edge

IMBOLC

*This path leads
To the solace of snowdrops.*

*The carpet of white is threadbare,
Cob webbed weavings
Of frozen water, seem to wait
A change of wind
To blow away.*

*Sunlight shivers
In the eastern sky,
And spreads across
The goose grey winter clouds.
But now, its strength
Begins to grow
With every turning of the earth,
Calls to the sleeping seed
To spite the ice,
And bring its blessing
To the waking world.*

*The milk of spring,
Begins to flow across the land.
The wind is changing.*

SPRING SONG

The deosil dance of the waxing year,
Brings the seed to birth,
As warmth drives out old winter's fear
And melts the heart of earth.

Raise up the lord of all that's green
And give him room to breathe,
Let him wake from winter's dream
To bless the budding leaves.

Let the maiden see her love
And greet him with a kiss.
Let them twine in oaken grove
To bring each other bliss.

Let earth and sun and wind and rain
Be fertile in their way,
As spring reclaims her old domain,
And life comes out to play.

MERRY MEET

*A lady walks the land,
Clothed in colours of the season,*

*A diadem of moonlight
Woven in her hair.*

*Her maiden gown,
Entrains;
The flowers of spring
Within the woods,
And wayside places.*

*Where she seeks her love,
The lord of all that's green.*

*Returning to her now
From a place of shadow,
Semblanced
In the likeness of a stag.*

SNOWING AGAIN

*So,
Winter's dug its claws in
Once again.
Polar Bear and Hare,
Circling.
But the stubble stag
Is stubborn;
Life already has
Too much flow,
For the snow
To stick for long.
This is just
A final parting kick,
From the old
Wild white wanderer
As he goes.
But Lop-ear
Just leaps
Across his toes
And powers through
The snow,
Shouting, GROW!*

HARE

Old brown lop eared one,
Spring is shaped
Within your form
And march wind madness.

Stubble stag jack,
Carrying full moon
Lunacy in the gleam
Of your eye.

Getting punch drunk
On summer's promise.

You run around
The flat, fat fields,
A whirling dervish,
Delivering dreams.

SPRING MORNING

Above, below,
Within
The misty
Growing green
Of Spring,
Birds sing their dreams
To the rising Sun;
While
Small brown bees
Float
Like amber motes
Upon the breeze;
Taking shots of gold
From the dandelion
Pots of old
Rainbows.

SPRING DAZE

*Streams of sunlight
Pour
From broken clouds.
The air sizzles
With mozzies.*

*Beech leaves
Teach the butterfly
To dance
On the breeze.*

*Tree shadow
Hides
A hollow way.*

*Emerald flecks
Flicker
In the deep dappled
Shadows.*

*Heartsease
Holds a grove of grace
Within the hedgerows' trove
Of root and briar.
Grey and gibbous rain clouds
Swim
Before the whale song wind.*

OSTARA

*This path leads
To a house without a key.*

*Old winters ice hard hand,
Now warmed and softened
By the light of spring,
Nurtures all the life
That's brought to birth*

*Trees delight;
The tingle
Of unfurling leaves.*

*The shadow
Of a bird in flight,
Sweeps in silent blessing,
Over budding branches.*

*Hare and moon,
Exchange a loving glance;
Then step the dance
That brings
The summer in.*

SPRING AND LEAP

A hare runs athwart the hill.
The moon is bright above the bay,
Breasting through
The silver waves of night.
The tide is turning,
Rolling in towards the shore,
White horses, galloping
Towards the longest day.

HOLLOW WAY

Listen to the misty whispers of the wood,
The ghostly voice of all its ancient roots;
Tread the brown leaf ground of mast and mold,
As calling crow, cracks open winters door;
Climb the mound, where once the oak tree stood,
Until its ancient roots gave up their hold
On earth and laid it down to life anew;

Watch where beauty spirals up
Each springtime stalk and stem;
Look where birch boughs reach
Like silver threads up to the sky;

Fly with the heron as she sweeps
In brief eclipse across the sun;
Wander where the streamlet winds,
While dreaming of the sea;
See beyond the shadows
Shaped by sunlight through the leaves;

Walk with the blossoming thorn,
Follow the unfurling oak,
Welcome the Goodman green,
Who pipes the seasons turn,
Beg a lift from burly Brock,
Along the hollow ways.

WANDERING

*(After an item on B.B.C. News about the slow death of
'purposeless' walking)*

*Wander lonely, like a cloud,
An aimless, gentle, breeze blown way,
Avoid the purposeful pressing crowd,
Just let your feet, pied piper play.*

*And walking, let your mind roam free,
To touch, then let the thought go far,
Let eyes not fix on what they see,
But lightly hold onto where you are.*

*Give no thought to journeys end,
Nor fear the ever-circling time,
Just see what intuition sends,
Or wait some serendipitous sign.*

*For this walk from place to place,
This idle, undirected drift,
Away from whirl of daily race,
May bring the grace of beauty's gift.*

SUMMER
Goddess,
In the wild wood,
Dancing for her stag love,
The joy of life within her heart,
Beating.

NE'ER CAST A CLOUT

It's a miserably drizzly, low visibility day,
The sky is a flat and featureless uniform grey,
There's an ache for the sun, that's felt deep down in the bones,
As the wind huddles by with a damp and rheumaticky moan.

The rain is a cobweb of cold that drifts on the air,
And slowly soaks into your skin, whatever you wear,
Each leaf that droops from the bough has a snivelling drip,
That drops down the back of your neck with a shivery slip.

The puddles that litter the path are deceptively deep,
And find their way into your shoes, with a saddening seep,
The ground is a churn of greasy and glutinous clay,
It's a miserably drizzly, low visibility day.

BELTANE

This path leads
To the birthing of the thorn.

On still cool mornings,
Sunlight turns the mist
To cloth of gold.

A stream of breeze
Splashes over rippling leaves.
And birds delight the clouds,
As they dance upon the air.

On the moss,
Guarding the gathering
Of the fae,
This May morning,
The gentle blessing
Of an aqua blue butterfly.

And in the branches,
The woven wonder
Of a birds' nest,
Built of love;
And mosswebs.

SUMMER SONG

The serenade of summer fills the air,
A harmony of sound and scent and sight,
Swift swooping swallows seem, without a care,
To launch headlong into the dazzling light;

The days eyes gaze on darting damselfly,
The meadows fill with bees' sweet honey drone,
Now all that's green, is open to the sky,
And whispers words that tingle in our bones;

An old enchantment carried on the breeze,
Of subtle, secret, aromatic spells,
Written by the sunlight, on the leaves
Of the ever-turning tale that nature tells.

FORGOTTEN FLOWERS

*I love the flowers
That fend for themselves, in wayside places,
That grow against the grain
Of bricks and mortar,
Ungrim, the grimy
Ground with gentle faces;
No matter
That the cubic feet of concrete,
Stride across the earth.*

*Careless of rough
Or scuff of uncouth boot,
The root grows tireless out,
To seek around each stone
And find a sip, a drip,
So, beauty spirals up each stalk and stem,
To push aside
The tarmac flat, city track; or re-seed
The dead tree roof.*

*They blur the line between the here and there;
Wilding the cracked and crumbled edge
Of the urban ubiquity.*

ROADSIDE

Blackheath on a cool summer's morning,
And a roadside caff for the bees,
There's vetch and bugloss vying
With poppies and plantain, to please.

A place of mallow and sun spurge,
Alongside the local bus route,
Where cornflowers grow on the grass verge,
And there's beetles in emerald suits.

A place for the crow kind to gather,
To 'murder' a good nutty feast,
And there's really no need to go further,
In search of more exotic beasts.

The Serengeti of south east London,
Just right for safari daytrips,
And if you're caught by the monsoon season,
There's a shop that sells fish and chips!

BEE

*I saw your tiny corpse,
Forgotten on the pavement,
A flash of shadowed gold
Brushed by the breeze.*

*Worn out,
By your unceasing search
For sweetness.*

*So, I laid you to rest
Among the flowers,
Knowing they will mourn you,
Better than I.*

SUMMER SHOWER

The summer shower's passed,
And through the field
A crystal crown of glitterati blooms
Raise up their face,
To show the place the rainbow's born.

A cacophony of colour,
Look at me, look at me, look at me, me, me;
It seems a swathe of every shade that's seen
Between the rise and set of sun and moon,
Against grass glinting emerald green
To silver sheen,
Now arcs across this land bound curve;

These miraculous motes
Like some impressionist daydream,
Blown by waves of wind,
Are escaping up the hill,
As if they would
Engulf the woodland shore
That holds the crest;
And burst the bounds of possibility.

LITHA

*This path leads
To the song of dreaming woods.
The many blessings
Of the sun
Are long remembered
In the roots of trees.*

*But deep within
The emerald dappled glades
Of oak and ash and thorn,
There waits a sylvan magic,
Where tales and visions
From the shadow lands
Between the dark and light,
May sometimes last
Beyond the bounds
Of shortest night.*

*While in the circle
Of the standing stones,
The sunlight pauses,
Warming earth's old bones;
As if unwilling to obey,
The distant call of shortest day.*

PUCK

Hedgerow Halfling,
Born of two worlds
With a dancing foot in each.

Feasting on the fruits
Of hazel tree and hive,
Quaffing foaming acorn cups
Of beer and buttermilk.

Shadow hopping
In a mouse skin cloak.
Or, riding through the night
Upon a barn owl,
You watch our ways
From season to season,
Within the circle
Of the passing year.

Your antlered alter ego
Slipping between the trees
On long mid-summer eves.

Spirit of both path and hearth,
You doze away the winter
Safe within the cob webbed corner
Of the Inglenook.

And have the greatest
love of humankind
Of all the folk who dwell
in hallowed hills.

An ancient Briton, brother to old Brock,
Riding on his burly back
Along the hollow track.

You counted Aveburys' standing stones
The day the builders left.
Helped to light the bonfires
That warned of Caesars might
And saw the fatal arrow
Find its mark on Senlac hill.

A woodland wisdom,
Green hearted, hooded man,
You were a force to count on
In those, straightforward days,
When there were more of you,
And less of us.

But then the cities grew,
And threw you back with all your kind
Out of mind,
Into our myth
And nursery rhyme.

And so we gave you,
In our foolishness,
A foxglove dunce's cap;
So we could laugh
Around our urban hearth,
At your madcap mischief.

And give no thought,
To what might lie,
Around the corner of our eye,
Within the darkling wood.

HEAT

On the beach,
Grains of proto glass
Glitter hot, stretching
Out across the dunes,
(That do not lack bottle)
Towards a sky
The colour of sand,
Where the sinking furnace,
Turns a flight of gulls
To seared silhouettes
And everything waits;
Upon the edge
And flow of quenching sea.

ESTUARY

The eye widens for lack of corners
In this long-lapped landscape,
Or squints, in squall of grit
Across the mud and marsh,
That stretches out
To where the sea
Becomes sky,
As far as the eye
Can see.

A semi liquid state, of salt and sand,
Washed by wandering inlets,
Which snake away
Through waves of sedge,
To where the waders dredge
The shifting edge.

This place of mists, shaping drifts,
Where water has a sweet and sour tang;
While the wind is ozone fresh,
Blown from the far horizon,
And a distant rush and roar
Reminds you, that sometimes
Nearer than you think,
Is the wild white sea herself.

SEA DREAMS

Sleeping,
On the edge of land;
The sea,
A sentient presence;

Wild white horses
Gallop
Through my dreams,
With eyes
As bright and deep
As ancient ice.

Stampeding mad
Along my shifting shore,
Set free
From Neptune's swelling stable,
Whipped up by sting of salt lash;
Selkies screaming
At their flanks to urge them on;
Yet ever
They flail and fall
To dusty, drowning death,
Beneath
The waiting sand.

AUTUMN

Goddess,
As the leaves fall,
Searching for her stag love,
She hears his call within the mist,
Fading.

AUTUMN MORNING

Rain;
Crackles the window,
Blown by a bluster
Of westerly wind;

The sun
Climbs up the trees,
Edging the clouds
In amber & sand;

The broken
Arc of a rainbow
Cracks
Open the sky;

Setting free
A dark sparkle
Of birds,
To speckle the grey.

LAMMAS

*This path leads
To the fields of rippling gold;*

*The summer lands
Of mouse and wren,
Must now go down
Before the scythe,
To make the bread
To break in celebration.*

*The harvest drives
The haunting thought
Of hunger
Far from hearth and home;
And brings a holiday
To bless the bounty
Of the earth.*

*The man of straw,
Who stood all summer long
With arms out flung,
May take his rest
Upon a stack of hay,
And know his job's well done.*

AUTUMN SONG

So comes the autumn waning of the year,
Light and life are drifting down to dusk,
Now all that's sown is grown and brought to barn.
And celebrations lighten evenings drear,
With merry maidens made from harvest husk,
And beer fermented long beneath the barm.

This time, when mornings have a smoky look,
And crows, like black kites, hang within the mist,
The trees float on the edge of winters sleep,
While bird and beast take shelter in their nooks,
And summer's laid to rest, within a kist
Of amber reminiscences, so deep.

The sun's bright strength is almost at an end,
The soil is strewn with early morning frost,
That seals the springtime deep within the ground.
And life must break, if life refuse to bend,
To sink, beneath the snowflakes fragile host,
There to wait the sunwise seasons round.

THE OWL

*A silent scythe
Of white wing
Cuts across the corn.*

*Athena's eyes,
Reflect
Diana's moon.*

*Fierce yet fragile
Feathered face;
Dowsing sound
Down to the merest
Mouse bite.*

HARVEST SONG

As the sunwise spiralling dance of days
Waxes and wanes with the year,
There falls a time when the lord of the fields
Must lay down his life again.
As his head goes down before the scythe
His spirit goes down to the Earth,
And the world is left to grieve a while
In darkness and in dearth.

May he find new strength in the Mothers' womb
And peace in her embrace,
Until time turns and he stands once more
Beside his maiden love.
May her sun lit smile as they pace the dance;
Make his old heart sing,
And his shining brow bring life and love
To the rise and blossom of Spring.

MABON

This path leads
To the wealth of bough and bush,
The burnished sunset of the year,
When nature wears her robes
Of autumn fire, and masks
Her fragile face with leaves of gold.

Apple cider scent brings
Celebrations incense
To barn and farm,
The gathered grace of mother earth,
Gives many gifts
To put aside the winters' wrath.
And make a revel of the bleakest time.

So, all may have the best of hope,
And sing the season on its way,
Good health, good cheer
Good food and beer;
Until the sun returns in spring,
To kiss the frost away.

THE OWL

A silent scythe

Of white wing

Cuts across the corn.

Athena's eyes,

Reflect

Diana's moon.

Fierce yet fragile

Feathered face;

Dowsing sound

Down to the merest

Mouse bite.

AUTUMN FROST

Frost.
Softer than breath;
This silver sighs away
Beneath a warming touch,

Leaving a tear
To trace across each leaf;
That it has lost
This last disguise of beauty,
And now
Must face the winter's dark,
And die.

Not knowing
Such bare bones as these,
Are full of wonder.

MIST

In the night,
The clouds reached down
To touch the earth,
And now a mist
Holds all in silent mystery.

The trees are overgrown
With grasping claws
That blindly grope at crying
Flying souls
The shape of crows.
Each root becomes
A goblins' trap to wrest the feet
From under the unwary.

The breath is thick and damp
Within the lungs
As if the air is filled
With cauls of cobweb.

And every sound
Of things unseen,
That slide and stalk
And circle round the ear;
Wake echoes weird and feared
Within the head.

BATS (a.k.a.) CHIROPTERA

Crepuscular chill
Of creeping mist.

From crook and crack
Of shadowed crag
Flicker flutter
Shivering shapes
Shake free.

To skip skitter skew
Across marsh and mere.

And catch
The erratic tracks
Of moths
With chittering clicks.

STAG

Woodland king, in the spring
Your breath lies softly
On the blessing of beginnings.

Watching from the twilight
Of the trees,
Your skin soft glimmers
Like a sunlit glade,
And your shape, shifts,
In the shadow changing
Of the branches.

Cousin of the Unicorn,
You step out softly to us
From the Otherworlds,
And in the deep, forested pools
Of your eyes,
We see our world,
Transformed and gentled.

Yet in the Autumn,
When sword and shield
Adorn and arm your brow,
And your challenge echoes
Off the Oak, to lesser mortals
Who would dare usurp you.

Then, you rip your realm
To ribbons,
To dress your fossil spears.
Then, you are the lustful lord

Of all the land,
The wild-eyed horned hunter.
Questing beast,

Your breath a scream,
That tears the leaves
From off the trees.
Your great heart crying
At the dying of the year.

AGAINST THE ODDS

*Howling like hornets
Round the cliff edge;
A whistling wail
Of weather breaks
The waves in a white hot
Whip lash salt stung crash
Against the shore,
That, raging back,
Sucks the sand
Down to drown
Beneath
Pounding white horse hooves.*

*Leaving Leached bare
Beach bones
Broken
By seaweed scars.*

*Black clouds
Crowd the rim of the world;
Lightning breaks
Their dark hearts.*

*Thunder drum rolls.
And then like rain,
The birds pour
From the night.*

*Wind swept scraps
Of burning Life;
Singing ancient song lines;*

*Winging in waves
Over the ocean.*

*Where each crest
Gives a knife edge,
To the pitch black,
Pitch Of the sea depths.;*

MOTHER OF THE DEEP

*Down in the deep
Dark swirl of salt sea greenness;
Gifting caviar
To the King at Reykjavik.*

*Sassuma Arnaa,
Weed maned she horse
Of the high white wave,
Sand pounder,
Fish giver,
Whale griever,*

*Wraps giant bones in
Salt cured kelp skin,
Breathes a bubbling
Rush of life
Into the blow hole,
To let them sing again.*

*Ululating through the
Undulating wave ways,
Telling tales
Beneath the green and shadowed branches
Of the World Tree,*

*That lays its light song
Across the white waves
Of the snow deep
Sea of land.*

*Where
Deer clad spear men
Stalk the thick skinned
Tusking Walrus.*

*Cut the skin
Of the world
To hunt within
Sassuma Arnaa's blood.*

*Or fly
Across her fathomless face
Within a seal skin nest,
To take the screaming sea birds
With stone barbed skill.*

*While the skin drum shaman
Dive into the dark green dream sea,
To seek their sins forgiveness
From the Mother of the Deep.*

WINTER

Goddess,
At the year's end,
Mourning for her stag love,
His spirit lies within the earth,
Waiting.

OTHERWORLD

Waking, one early winter dawn;
The setting moon
Rests between the western trees;
A ghostly echo of the call of owls.

The ground is covered with a silver skin,
That sculpts the shape of every ridge and fold
In fallen moonbeams.

While in the east,
The mist is spun by rising sun
Into a cloth of gold,
That hangs from bright edged boughs.

And where these skeins
Of shimmering earth and air were met;
In this between and waiting time;
Another world seemed set.

Where every tree was bowed
With leaf and fruit,
And meadows,
Where wild rainbows flowered,
Curved out across the hills;

Through folds of land,
A river ran; glittered
With the falling light of stars;

While in the emerald shadows
Of the woods,
The dappled deer stood watchful
Of the dawn.

These sights unwound
Within the drawing of a breath;
While sleeps still hand
Was resting, still, upon me.

Then the blackbird
Piped his bright aubade;
Sweet notes of light
To sing the moon to sleep

And all this otherworld
That seemed so real,
Was held within a dew drop;
Balanced,
On a blade of grass.

SAMHAIN

*This path leads
To a place beyond the dusk,
Where winter's winds sing softly,
And gently brush the veil
Of passing time.*

*Insubstantial mist
Of moonlight over all,
Gives gleam of gaunt lit silence;
Where shadows
Take a ghostly shape, that shifts
From each remembered moment.*

*A dreaming scape,
Where wisdom is
A whispered presence,
Heard beyond recall
Of earthly realms.*

*Communion of the then
And now, for knowledge
Of the new year
Yet to come.*

WINTER SONG

Stark the sight seems,
Iron hard the earth-hold of this solstice time.
The joy of seasons past, gone down to dust
Beneath the gasping grasp of cold.

The world, suspended in a snow drift,
Sleeps away the sun starved winter wait,
Water cracks beneath the weight of frozen air,
Trees stand withered in the north born wind;
Life is but a shudder of its former self.

Yet still the life persists,

The robin sings his song of hollow hills,
Fox tracks dance across the frosty ground,
Snowflakes whisper secrets as they fall,

The evergreen man still shows his face,
And listens
For the heart of mother earth,
That barely beats;
But does.

A DREAM OF SNOW

Bare;
Beneath the silence
Of the Owl's wing,
A land lies dreaming
Of the memory
Of movement.

While water
Holds its breath,
Below a haloed moon;
And clouds, like
Ancient ice floes,
Float on the currents
Of a midnight
Starlight sea.

WINTER EVENING

Dusk holds a certain smokiness.
The western sunken sun,
Shrouded in a dream of cloud,
Shines like a sliver of memory
From behind the hill.
Fields,
Floating in the shadow stream,
Swirl up the silent slope
To where the trees stand.
Silhouetted. Sentinel.
Gaunt the ground lies;
Woven in a web of frost fret,
Grass blades glimmer,
Shimmer in a sheath of rime.

Hunching, ancient hedgerows,
Those hoary old retainers,
Wander white-haired
On the field rim.
Water wears a shard-shield,
A crystal scintillation
Caught in creaking clamp of cold.
While in the east,
The iron-black, crackling sky,
Subtly softens
To a sable phosphorescence,
As the lustrous moon
And her sisterhood of stars,
Wake to watchfulness,
Above the sleeping Earth.

RAVEN

*Who is now coming back from the Atlantic "fringe"
to re-populate the land.*

HRAFN!

You old shaman.

Skilled in Galdorcraeft.

Sky-chanting ancient runes,

Shapeshifting in the void,

Wings weaving wyrd

Across the wind.

Namer of the landscape,

Keeper of thought and memory,

Dweller on the edge.

The old shaman is returning,

HRAFN!

RED KITES FEEDING

*The Ravens jump and skitter
In the field,
Strange to see such big birds
In a jitter,
Nervous of shadows,
They hop and skip away
From shapes above,
Trying to look every way.
At once,
Bowled over by the passing
Rush of wind
Into inelegant flap and fluster,
Rushing in and out to grab
A mouthful as they can;
With what courage they can muster,
In case some descending talon,
Should mistake them
For its lunch.*

MID-WINTER

When
In this darkest midnight of the year,
All is silent, slumbering,
Still.
Held fast at home
By winters wailing wyrd.

When
The hunter walks the heavens,
The wolf haunts the homestead,
And trees raise shrunken limbs
In supplication to the sleeping sun.

Then
The Raven
Shakes the moon embroidered silver
From his wing tips,
And, soaring upward
Through the graylag sky,
Chants the ancient spell of waking
To the frozen Earth.

Then,
A maiden,
Still sleeping snug
Beneath her snow-white blanket.
Begins to stir,
Dreaming of Stags;
And snowdrops.

YULE

*This path leads
To a hearth born hope of light.
The sun breaks free of winters icy wrath,
Unwraps the lengthening of days,
And gives the gift of life
Once more to earth.*

*Yet still, that bright brow
Gleams with untried strength,
And doubt remains
That it will stand the test.
That wind and ice
And mire of sleet, may bury deep
The unknown way,
And all conspire to lose
The lambent light,
Within the realm
Of drifting snow.*

*Yet deep within the white,
There glows the green,
And holly knows,
It must give way to oak.
That hidden in the depths
Of longest night,
There is a gleam of dawn.*

EVERGREEN

Now bring the evergreen to hearth and hall,
For see, the bold and brazen sun grows pale,
And all the world is wrapped in winter's pall,
Now bring the evergreen to hearth and hall.
For we must pray for light and life to all,
And give him strength by lifting loud wassail,
Now bring the evergreen to hearth and hall,
For see, the bold and brazen sun grows pale.

CRONE

She who circles standing stone,
Eyes a shadow in a skull,
She who sings the north wind's moan,
Watching Reindeer, counting cull.

She who drums the earth to life,
Cuts the cord of all that's born,
She who is the spring's midwife,
Brings to bud the antlered thorn.

She who stands outside the hearth,
Wrapped within a crystal cloak,
She who walks the moon's bright path,
And waits; beneath the old grey Oak.

She who gives her ancient blood,
To brightly bless the winter king,
And in whose heart is understood,
The silent song the menhir sings.

Life and death, blood and bone,
Walk the track, old grey stone,
Sing the song, journey home,
Antlered Maiden, Mother, Crone.

SOLSTICE

Silent, secret, sylvan shadows,
Slip between the winter trees.
There comes a sound like distant drumming,
Carried on a rustling breeze.

A figure walks the dreaming trackways,
Through this ancient forest night.
A woman, pale as silver birch bark,
Dressed in gown of purest white.

She steps from out the trees dark shadow,
Into a glade of frost touched turf.
Her footfall leaves no print upon it,
She is the moon; come down to earth.

Within this landscape wreathed in magic,
Walks another maiden fair.
Clothed in robes of green and amber,
Oak leaves woven in her hair.

Given form by earth's great spirit,
Come to meet her moon born kin.
Her eyes are bright as rain washed berries,
Like summers wild rose is her skin.

They meet within the trees soft circle,
Greeting with a sisters kiss.
Then stand and watch towards the pole star;
There is a third, that yet they miss.

And time is held between two moments,
Like the pause within a breath.
Or like, that infinite quietus,
That seems to wait upon a death.

The other comes on steps of silence,
Dressed in robes of Raven black.
A coldness, worse than any winter,
Follows fast upon her track.

A cowl enshrouds the ancient features,
Of this dark unseelie she.
A face of cruel and harsh uncaring,
That mortal eye would dread to see.

She is the Hag, midwinter's spirit,
Collector of the seasons due.
Those lives, demanded by the north wind,
To let the spring be born anew.

She steps into the star lit clearing,
Moves her hand above the ground.
A mist arises from the frost fret,
Begins to drift the circle round.

Within this icy breath of winter,
These spirits tread a sunwise path.
Creating with their slow progression,
A timeless, placeless, hallowed garth.

A space for them to work their wisecraft,
Where the drumming louder grows.
And where, like ice, so slowly melting,
The time once more begins to flow.

Quicker now their footsteps falling
As they weave the world afresh,
Their forms, so ghostly in the mist light,
Seem to shimmer, shift and mesh.

Round in sunward sacred circle
Three in one the figures flow
The heartbeat drumming of the season
Deep within the ground below

Then; all is gone from in the clearing,
Except the mist drifts deosil,
It spirals, wanders, weaves and falters,
Stops; and all is utter still.

Faint the sound of drumbeat fading,
Lingers on the cold night air,
The mist, performs one last enchantment;
Unveils the figure standing there.

This shortest night draws to its ending
As golden glimmers edge the Earth,
And from this charm of solstice making,
The form of spring is given birth.

A maiden, fair as season's blessing,
As golden haired as harvest dream.
Her gown is like a May day meadow,
A sunrise sown in every seam.

She looks towards the days new dawning,
Her skin is washed in pearly light
Her eyes reflect the east's pale colour,
She trembles like the lark in flight.

She is the gift of ancient spirits,
She is the wise craft that they send,
She is the new life of the season,
She is the gold at rainbows end.

She walks towards the forests welcome,
She steps in wonder, like a fawn.
Beneath her feet, the world is breathing,
As all that's green is now re-born.

She reaches to the trees bare branches,
At her touch, the leaves unfurl.
She smiles to see this gentle magic,
And walks into the waking world.

Silent, secret, sylvan shadows,
Slip between the springtime trees.
There comes a sound, like pan pipes playing,
Carried on a whispering breeze.

AFTERWORD

When I have done with this old shell of mine,
And all my atoms start to come apart,
I will not grieve the passing of my time,
When I have done with this old shell of mine.
For molecules, forever, re-align;
And may form yet another beating heart
When I have done with this old shell of mine,
And all my atoms start to come apart,

So, this was me...Martin, or Moonie to my friends. Pagans and alcohol - what can I say? I lived on the drifting edge of Epping Forest in North East London where I wrote poetry and short fiction inspired by nature, folklore, and my animist beliefs. I was an actor for a lot of years but later I just performed my own stuff when the opportunity presented itself (this  *may also have involved Pagans and alcohol strangely enough!). I have been published both online and in print; in the U.K. and America and was featured in the anthology Moon Poets; but this is the second book that's entirely my own.*
  Bright Blessings.

ALL ROYALTIES FROM THIS BOOK GO TO BATTERSEA CATS AND DOGS HOME.
Printed in the UK by CLOC Book Print
clocbookprint.co.uk

A LITTLE SPACE FOR YOUR THOUGHTS & INSPIRATIONS

www.ingramcontent.com/pod-product-compliance
Lightning Source LLC
Chambersburg PA
CBHW071537080526
44588CB00011B/1706